The Observer

Tony Prewit

The Observer
© Tony Prewit, 2014 all rights reserved
Published by Ridgeline Press
Silver City, New Mexico, U.S.A.
ISBN 978-0-9854487-7-6

Editing, book design, cover design, and production services by Heidi Connolly, Harvard Girl Word Services
Cover artwork by Tony Prewit

Acknowledgments

I would like to thank my wife, Patricia Prewit, for the years of assistance in sorting, editing, and proofreading all my work. I thank her most of all for being her and allowing me to continue to be the person she married. I would also like to thank my editor, Heidi Connolly, who helped with the sculpting of this book. Her vision, talent, and professional guidance have been invaluable.

Other Books by Tony Prewit

Six-book Series: *Journey in the Mind's Eye of a Poet*

>   *Journal of Time*
>   *Portals and Passages*
>   *The Book of the Lost and Found or Chasing Rainbows*
>   *Moods of War*
>   *The Source*
>   *Another Day*

Spiritual Travelers . . . on our own without a map

Table of Contents

Introduction

I, an observer of life, share these images of life with the hope that they offer lessons in life as well.

The observer learns to listen to those around him.
Whether in body, mind, heart or spirit, listening is the key.

I therefore record what I hear and pass it on to you.

Set the World Right

1.
without reason or authority
other than being born a poet.

2.
i consider the world in present
past and future to be spiritual

where there is dark i see light
where there is light i see dark

all that is hidden i must find
of all that is seen i must be sure

i am driven by secrets
i see morality as a prisoner

as the world collides with spirit
i am there as an observer.

3.
the journey for the poet is measured
not in worldly but spiritual ways

where the mission is to set
the world right

to convince a poet otherwise
is to believe one can convince
the sun not to rise

a poet not made by choice
but through self-discovery

born to write
born to shed light.

Rule to Live By

if we live by
the rule
that says
to ourselves
be true

we
will soon see
a mirror
of our
own morality

—mirror mirror
on the wall

but if we live
by the rule
that says all
are equal in
how
they should
be treated

then we have
the answer
to the question

—what do You require of me my God.

I Am (One)

if i were an island
and i had sun
rain wind
and all kinds of
living creatures
and plants

   i would have everything i would need

but if one day
i looked beyond
the horizon and
saw another
island

   would i still be content

the first moment
i saw you i knew
i needed you
in my life

even an island
like me
needs to share
its sun rain
wind and all
that it has

   you were the unmaking of the island i had created in myself.

I Am (Two)

1.

i am
power

i am
savior

i am
heat

i am
cool

i serve
i rule

i am
peace

i am
fear

i am
uranium seed

i am
the worst of need

i am radio–
active

i am that i am.

2.
i am a dream
i am a nightmare

i am breath
i am death

i am the way
to the last day

i am the shallow of
humanity's creativity

i am that i am
—and i am nuclear.

Duel

1.
where are you my *evil* son
where are you my *good* son

inside my soul i fear
which son today will i hear

i am a father who cares for both
my sons equally and impartially.

2.
take her
devour her
and then take
several more if you want

or

love her
caress her
as your only one
and show her you care.

3.
devise a plan
where you amass wealth
fill your tents with your every desire

or

like a good servant
seek where there is a need
and offer help when you can.

4.

my son *evil* and
my son *good*

both have need
of me
and i have need
of them

out as twins they came
and brought me joy
but now i see
they are twins
only in that they were
born together
and are
different as
night and day

in public
i love them equally
but in private
i am forever choosing

and they
endlessly fighting
for my favor.

5.
we are hollow observers
we stare at ourselves empty
not understanding the never-ending fight
within us

every human births
these twins

at odds with each other
always ready for a duel

> *better to die in a duel*
> *this way*
> *they say than to give in*
> *to the other*

we all bear the two children
of our soul
and bear the burden
they bring.

If the Dreams

1.

if all our dreams came true all the time
would chaos reign in the universe

what if we dreamed of perfect harmony
what then

come you prayer
bring peace
bring harmony
to every dream.

2.

i dreamed i was in boat with thousands
of people when a mist came over us

within the mist we each lived in our own world
without disturbing the other's

if invited to join another's world we were
polite guests and they were polite hosts

> *i love the mist*
> *of this dream*
> *it is my drug*
> *of choice.*

3.
can we make ourselves disappear from the
world we know

and enter into what we imagine to be the
best world of all

> *if for a moment*
> *we loosen the cord*
> *that binds our imagination*
> *what kind of world would we create*
> *and what kind of dreams*
> *would we dream*
>
> *can truth be found in a land*
> *sowed by imagination and dream.*

In Silence

1.
i am silenced
by me
for what i saw
in me
was
a false humility

which once
seen
became
an embarrassment

now i am seeking
the quieter
way
rather than the
way of
boastful claims

to not say whatever
comes to mind
no matter how clever

being silent
is a challenge
i am
unaccustomed to.

2.
silence is
recreating
me

i am learning the
grateful

i am learning the
still

though
i have many
thoughts
i would like to speak
only a few
matter

> *my silence*
> *within*
> *has become*
> *where the re-creation*
> *of me begins.*

I Am Done

i am done with yesterday
my vision of myself has moved me on

it's not that i've found myself
        but rather that i've changed
as i searched

perhaps i've spent
        too much selfish time
as the world
        evolved

as i've aged a new awareness
        of myself has emerged
i see clearly that every vision
        needs change

so i've allowed myself to change
        and not hold on
to the dead vines of yesterday.

Journeys In

One—

where do
life and
i fit

is it a
risk to
search
for where
one
belongs

we
all do it
as if searching
were
meant to be
and
started at
birth.

Two—

my hand
reaches
for
yours

though
invisible
it may
be
to you

my hand
still reaches
for
yours.

The Observer

Three—

stained glass
marble carvings
hardwood pews
compare not to
hillsides
where the eye
can see
for miles
and where
horizons
rise out
of dust
like visions

my God
is more
real to me
on a hillside
than in
cathedrals
no matter
how much
cathedrals
are
admired

air
on the
hill
is better
breathed

as it
seems
there is more
of God
here
than in
the air
encased
in a marble
fortress

but i
must say
to each
his
own
where
God is
concerned

i give you
your need
of how you
need God

i ask you
to give me
the same

and if we
see we
are equal
to God
here

then
whether
in cathedrals
or on hills
will we
then see
with the
eyes of
God.

Questions for Gods

why does morality
need a conscience

why do memories
need peace

why do followers need leaders
why do leaders need followers

why a sunrise and sunset
why light and dark

why have we created
so many images of God

why do we never see
war as other than the answer

how many gods does it
take to answer our questions

how many believers does it
take to create a god.

Quiet My Soul (One)

quiet my soul

talk not
just to
be heard

let go
the noisy
spirit
and it will
leave.

Quiet My Soul (Two)

i look up
and see
only sky

> i fear
> God is
> not what
> i imagined

> *quiet my soul*

> God created
> sky and all
> that is seen
> and unseen.

Quiet My Soul (Three)

i see
no god
on earth i
can trust

      is God
      not to be
      grasped
      but
      to be
      imagined
      and
      known only
      in spirit

      quiet my soul.

What Are the Odds

this morning
a whirlwind
came through
my camp
causing chaos

what are the odds

the old testament
writers believed
God was in the
whirlwinds

what are the odds

i looked out
over the hills
and down the
dry meadow
where i was
camped

i imagined being
an old testament
prophet and having
a whirlwind come
upon me

how where and
why we see God
as we do seems

to change with
the times and culture
and wind

    what are the odds.

Why Would God Punish Me for My Sin

1.
i look in the mirror
and all i see of me
is skeleton

my flesh sagging
my soul gone
i let them starve
for the fear of Hell
looming over me

i am but thirteen years
and the idea of
over–weight is
like a devil
laughing
yet i follow its will

this question hangs over me
like a shadow with fangs
why would God
punish me for
my sin

if i jump who would care
if i shoot myself who would care
if i swallow the whole bottle who would care.

2.
i am images of someone
else's belief
i starve myself as if
their slave

>   how did fat become
>   my doom where my all
>   is consumed by it
>   alone
>
>   why would God punish the fat
>   but not the thin.

3.
who thought it up that God
rewards and punishes

and why do we follow
meekly

the way is dark and
the path is rocks

but we march onward

we fall in line like
lambs

> *if i die before i wake will they say*
> *God surely punished her*
> *she was wafer thin and*
> *we all know God*
> *hates wafer*
> *thin.*

4.
i will open myself up today and
write of this in my journal

if tomorrow a stranger reads
of my journey and it stirs
a truth i know not of

will my thoughts have
value beyond my pain

will the dark rocky path where
hell leads offer some
comfort therein

if i hunger and choose its death
and in my defeat save another
is my starvation not in vain

this conviction moves me toward
permission to allow myself
my addiction

> *now at rest i ask with resolve*
> *why would God*
> *punish me for*
> *my sin.*

5.

if i helped one person
but perished in my own
despair

is saving another from my sin
the path to understanding
mercy

and is mercy the power
of forgiveness

if so i look for God there
to have mercy on my
self-starvation
and fear of
fat

i rest my case
and am now willing
to erase the question

> *why would God*
> *punish me for*
> *my sin*

if i die from a shallow fear will my death reach
the depth of others who may seek to follow me

will i be able to lift them from where i go
and persuade them to abandon my folly

sincerely
a thirteen-year-old.

Day-moon Type

i am a day-moon type

>*rarely acknowledged*
>*but there*

>*you have to pause to*
>*look for me*

>*and if you do—no guarantee*
>*you will see.*

Bad Dream

how do i let her go
and make it right
the woman i have loved
for forty-three years

i see her linger with
        new friends and
hesitate when she is with me
        as if she prefers
them over me
        yet she has committed
to me

how do i let love take
        its course
if i am loved by her
        it will be her choice
if not
        i will burden her
no more

        the loss would be a better pain
        than the constant gnaw in me
        watching her linger with new friends.

Love Like This

1.
her love
lights
my life
with
her smile

her beauty
stirs
my soul
to follow
with my
eyes

her motion
is like
a motif
compelling
me
to her.

2.
we
have in
each
other
what we
always
wanted
in a com-
panion
what
more
would
satisfy
me.

3.
if this
love is
lost
then
its value
will
multiply
and
steal
my soul
away

*i cannot
describe it
adequately*

*it is a love
that must
be ex-
perienced
to be
known*

*when a love
lights your
life with
only a smile
you will
know the love
i have.*

Two Observations of the Three Dogs' Owner
From my chair at the espresso coffee bar

One . . .

the idea of a person for all seasons
at first seems
shallow

but as i watch the owner
practice this
art

i can see that perhaps
there is more
depth

than i had assumed there to be
in that kind of
soul

for he makes the effort
to befriend
all

and to touch upon any
subject his clients
desire

i humbly bow to him
a person for all
seasons

he has traveled inner
depths i know
not of.

Two . . .

the establishment and vision of the owner
is a twenty-by-twenty room
—maybe a bit larger
but not by much

brick and plaster
a screen door with
a solid wood
counter

a few tables with pipe
legs and solid wood
bench seats

—this is three dogs
espresso coffee
bar

every glass of coffee
close to perfect

most likely the best espresso
in town and

probably for 100 miles in
any direction

people come and go
the room is full then
empty then full
again and
again

conversations are as varied
as wildflowers
in a field

and the depth of their words as
shallow and as deep as
each listener perceives
them to be

—*all are welcome at*
three dogs espresso
coffee bar

i frequent three dogs
and have noticed
one other thing

the owner is genuine
kind to everyone
treating all with
equal respect

—*i could be wrong about this*
but i do not think so.

Spirit Path

the path is not
always clear
nor the reasons
why we take the
path we do

the way of the
spiritual road
is new to
each of us
as we make
our way

as we journey
there will be
stories to
tell and
mysteries that
unfold

so whether
free or bound
rich or poor
with many
or alone

if the path of
our spirit has
no boundaries
other than
those we
impose

if our spirits
breathe free
and are
assigned to
guide us
from
conception
to eternity

*—and if
our spirit
waits
for us
to come
to seek
the path
that
was created
for us*

*then why
do we
hesitate.*

Strange

it was thirty years since we'd talked
then suddenly as i crossed
the narrow back street he saw me
and stopped beside me
in his 1972 red ford truck
half-ton

he said i hear you retired
i said yes how about you
i have nine more
years as a janitor at the
high school he said

then he laughed and said that's right
i never left
then slowly he drove away saying
it was good talking to
you again

i watched his red ford turn the corner
not knowing if we would ever
converse again

—strange
i vaguely remembered him
but evidently he had remembered me
from high school

i admire his memory and
friendly approach
i had not developed as well as he
in that regard.

Odd Thing

one day i was hiking up a mountain trail
as a man was coming down the trail
we both paused a moment to
exchange these words as we
walked past
each other

he said
i take my pistol when i go hiking
        i said *oh*

he said
i shoot the fish
it's easier than fishing

        i said *oh*

as we parted ways
he added one last comment

i am buddhist

then he continued his hike down the trail
and i resumed my hike up the trail thinking

        odd how
        it was that i'd never connected
        killing fish with a pistol
        to buddhism.

Our Love Never Happened

i loved her
but she did not
love me

i waited and i
schemed and i
tried

and
she ignored
me

marrying three
times

her memory has
faded

our love never happened.

The Life of . . .

the
life
of the
flesh
is
flesh

the
life
of the
mind
is
mind

the
life
of the
heart
is
heart

the
life
of the
spirit
is
spirit

> *and all*
> *of the above*
> *are the*
> *life of*
> *me.*

Water Came Rushing

water came rushing over the rocks
and through the canyon
sound echoed
against the
canyon
walls

reminding me of my love for you when we first met.

Note for Young Lovers

embrace young lovers
move your arms and hands
and legs and bodies up against
one another

let this altar of love be built

though it can be as elusive
as desert sand

though it shifts and it blows and never
gives solid ground

still love has a chance
to last forever

> *to fill our soul by the mere memory*
> *of loving at least once without*
> *thought of tomorrow.*

Back

there was an artist dedicated and motivated at
a young age to paint and write and play music
he was good at all these creative endeavors
—those around him who were not
did not understand

pressured to go to business school to
pursue a career to make money
—that is what the young
artist did

after thirty years the young artist had grown older
and wiser and richer than he believed possible
retiring at fifty he began again to pursue
artistic endeavors

though much time was lost it did not take long
for the creativity to flow once more

i was curious to know what might have been had
this artist pursued his creative side rather than
a business career

he told me he was glad that that he had made the
decisions he did for he could now pursue
the artist's life without economic
pressure

he added that other artistic people like him who did not
pursue careers with monetary rewards were often
pressured by needs later in life that
caused them much grief

i asked him which is better—to put off the dream and risk
losing it for financial freedom or pursue the dream
and take the risk of living in poverty

he said *you decide . . . my way worked well enough
i am back and i am glad and my creativity is
flowing . . .*

*decisions are not without risks . . .
it is the risks we choose that play
a huge part . . . .*

What If

what if shakespeare were born in america in 1954
what would he have become

what if hitler were born a black slave in 1829
what would he have become

what if aristotle were born in germany in 1904
what would he have become

do time and circumstance play a part in shaping
our destiny as well as our dna

let's play in this field of *what ifs* . . . if only for the reason
that it leads us to conclusions previously unconsidered
just in case we find the new conclusions
useful
  —what if.

Rejection

my worth as a human
is determined
by what i deem its worth
to be

without some vision
of self-worth
i fear i would reject
myself

and then others
would form
the same opinion
of me.

The Dark Side to Peace

if we have discovered peace at all
it is knowing it has two sides

the respect we want from others
needs to be given first
and then peace will allow us rest
to sleep without fear

    but there is a dark side

if we incite fear in others and imply
that their life is a risk to our own
unrest gives cause for sleepless nights

when the defeat of others becomes
our answer to peace
and believing that life without those we fear
will bring us rest

    fear has become our guide

if we inflict many wounds and
make enemies for life
we are on the dark side of peace

though at first it may seem light
the more we follow

    the darker the light becomes.

Revelation Worth Considering

i am waking and it is about 4:00 a.m.
i am somewhere between
wake and sleep

in a dream i see my parents
i watch them from a distance
they are cold and alone

they have climbed to the top of a mountain
and now have nowhere else to go
the path stops there

they look around for others to
bring them shelter and food

myself and others come to them
and we misinterpret their chill
and fear as if we are meant
to comfort them

but as i watch the scene the more i see
that we are supposed to delay so that
they may not look to us

but rather contemplate what it is that
brought them there and to see
the reality of fate

i see beyond the mountain
the place where we all must
journey

after we reach the top
—the top of the mountain is
the jumping off place

> *all of us must make the jump*

no one can prevent another's jump only interfere
and how do we justify this intrusion
—we name it *compassion*

without a vision of the mountain and why
our compassion only produces more pain
and guilt to both giver and receiver

but the pain of the jump off the top of the mountain
is only a moment and all fear and pain
is lost after it is over

but to intrude upon the jump in guise of compassion
—is this compassion without vision and
compassion ill-used

to allow the jump or delay the jump
—for what purpose

as i wake from my dream my parents' image fades
a chilling fearful dream but lined in truth

> *we fear our own inevitable fate for we are without vision of*
> *how to proceed once we reach the top of our mountain*
> *and so leave our fate to others*

> *when is it time to take the time to seek a vision for our life*
> *beyond this one.*

Gust and a Shadow

like a short gust
that disrupts
a quiet day

and then quickly
goes along its way

like a shadow that is here
for a short while

and then dissolves

you come into my life
with flare and
ambiguity

what am i to think

a gentle breeze
over an autumn
afternoon
i can fall in love
with

and shadows from clouds
and trees that
move gradually over
grassy hills

but you are not this
kind of moving
specter

The Observer

for you want my love
only in your
transient
need

and this i cannot do

how can i be content
with only infatuation
and the heat of the
moment

> though i feel there is
> more to your flare
> than you are willing
> to give
>
> and there is more
> to your depths
> than you are willing
> to share
>
> being that i could wait
> without knowing how long
> would i be willing to take the risk
>
> i may cave before you give in to my need
>
> will we ever learn to love more simply
>
> if only love were more simply.

Call of My Spirit

the call of my spirit

opens the

i-ing

my mantra

sings

the call of my spirit

breathes

within

where

time

ceases

and

i-ing

travels

paths

where

The Observer

mystery

calls out

to truth

and

in

silence

truth

speaks

while

chanting

"i-ing"

my mantra

sings

as a

silent

spring

rolling

over rocks

of the

river

in my

soul.

Death by Numbers

death—
why does
she follow
me
and lure
me
to gaze upon
her

i want not her
prize
yet i am drawn
in
as if i have
no
choice

born to
seek her
not
through
age
or disease
or accidentally
but with
a secret
zeal

to grow old
is my fear

age
an empty
breath

do i
wait for
death
to wear out
my life
or

do i
seek her
as a
lover
would
and run
to her
with
arms
out-
stretched

will my
epitaph
read as
a love true
or
a tragedy
and a
ruin

though
she is
spoken of

cruelly
and
forever
misjudged

i see her
as a lover
waiting

i go
to her
as a victor
who has
found love

> *my darling*
> *my death*
> *i have kept*
> *you waiting*
> *long enough.*

Future Me

solar x
warm neurons
pathways to
comfort
my sensation
of cold

serum code
calculates pulse rates
and sends a mess-
age to
my aging meta-
bolism
to slow down
and live a long
productive life

physics 21
mirror to my image
into me
i am one with
thee
programed
for eter-
nity
without
proof.

The Greatest of Privileges

who can reason
to convince
us

that to choose
when to
die

is as much a
victory as
life

where is the counselor who
can convince
us

that we need to choose our death
and burden not the
living

the way i die and the time i die
and the encouragement to make the choice
is the greatest of reasons not to fear life
or death and know there is a time
for both

> *to have this choice without judgment or restraint*
> *is the greatest of privileges.*

The Chase

i chased
you

you
chased
me

until one
of us
caught
the
other

and
gave
in
to the
other's
desire

      and
      now
      without
      the chase

      giving
      in is
      not
      the
      same.

The Lake

i began my usual walk to the lake one day and came upon

    a barbed-wire fence with a no trespassing sign

i soon discovered the fence surrounded the lake

    with only a single entrance to the water

and that there were fees and permits and other barriers barring us

    humans from getting too close

who had done this

    who had impeded our entrance to the lake

—the lake was my solitude
a place to go to walk or sit and be free to inquire
to find peace in my choices in life

and the barbed-wire around the lake reminds me why i left
the organized religions of the world
that restricted my freedom of solitude choice and peace

it could be argued we need some barbed wire in our lives
as well as free access to the lake

so what we are left with is one of the on-going historically
unresolved paradoxes of human nature.

The Way Through

traffic
    life
watch
    signs
move
    along

life changes
if we do not
heed the signs
blame not
others

i waited
and what
i waited for
never came
but age
did

a wise person
once said
    age is
    the part of life
    that is certain
    all else is random
    so
    do not wait
    rather
    live
    each day

The Observer

traffic
      life
watch
      signs
move
      along.

Title Page

i thought i
could create myself
in the image
i wanted

i was wrong

but i did not know
that until years
later

the title page
being my name
confused
me

i thought i was
supposed to
know the
meaning
of the
title page
before i
moved
on

and that
is where
life got
me

i was too
caught up
in the
title page
you
see.

Peace Comes with Scars

A vision of a lost love—crashing to earth

      1.
the gently rolling hills
and the afternoon
cool breeze
wrapped
me in
their
arms

the smell of wildflowers
and the scent of
the morning
rain soothed
my weary
bones

        i thought this moment
        could last
        forever

        i had never had
        peace like
        this

        time became timeless
        i felt light and i felt
        beautiful.

2.
as i rolled along on this
country road
my bicycle seemed not
to touch ground

then a shadow crossed over
the hills and waited
for me on the
path

i moved through its darkness
and as i did the feeling
of the joy of the day
faded

>my chance at love
>led me to a high
>place past the
>hills
>
>and now a shadow
>was following me close
>behind
>
>i left the high place
>and wandered
>through a dry
>creek
>
>the sun became hot
>i found shade
>and lay
>against the
>tree and
>slept.

3.
i woke from a dream and found myself
lying at the edge of a cliff

beside me lay my bicycle
rims bent and tires flat

i was unsure how i had arrived
at the cliff's edge

and how long i had been
lying there

i remember in my dream i was rubbing
my hands across my arms

and feeling an unfamiliar
coarseness

and seeing scars all over
my body

in my dream i knew these scars
were an image of my soul

        —*scars left by lost love.*

4.
i heard a distant wind shouting
through the canyon below

and then gradually a breeze embraced
me and with it came
a peace

      my scars were many
      but a salve had been applied
      to soothe my ache

      but as i began to heal
      i saw the scars would
      remain.

5.

i see now that a love door had opened
and i'd walked through it

a joyous abandonment
greeting me there

as i'd traveled along this road through
its gentle hills i'd suddenly crashed

illusions of a moment in time had caught me
unaware of the rocks in the road

i thought the moment of this new love
would last forever

but i'd hung in the balance unknowing that
the ground i was on was mere loose sand
and gravel

though my wounds since have healed
my scars remain

—*there to remind me.*

6.
after some time passed i was determined
to return to the spot of my crash

i ventured back to the cliff's edge
i walked back through the
dry creek and over the
meadows and
rolling
hills

i saw where my bicycle had once lain

the memory of the crash
has faded

the strength of the shadow
has been sapped

   —*my scars have made me strong.*

7.
i have shown my scars
to my friends

to my surprise they cannot
see them

they see only clean flesh
lean and tanned

i am unconvinced by what they do not see

though i see the scars

      —i am at peace.

A Better Way

i imagined i connected with God
and that He suddenly changed my life
but my "changed" life did not impress anyone
as being one of someone who had connected with
God and had an immediate life–
changing experience

only in small doses does real change occur
to believe otherwise makes us a bore

i think i would be better off becoming
a better me over time rather than
convincing myself of a faith that imagines
a sudden connection to God that enacts
a swift improvement in my life.

> *i know this statement will not appeal to those who prefer*
> *the idea that faith can change one's life in an instant*
>
> *but i see it as more real when it is a faith in oneself*
> *that opens a path to finding change and meaning*
> *rather than trusts in a faith where God*
> *instantaneously does the work for you*
>
> *my life has been transformed by believing in my own will*
> *and its power to change and give meaning to my life*
>
> *my will being the part of me in which God ministers*
> *and encourages me to move on*

—it is the path i have followed
it is where i have found my faith in God

perhaps faith does not have to be the same for everyone
for it to be faith.

Clips

1.

the deal is—

God has made no real commitment to us

therefore we all get away with murder

eternally speaking

we are left to punish and reward ourselves and make

and enforce the rules as to who rules for

as long as we are on the

earth.

2.

the mirror revelation is—

one day i saw that the compassion i extended toward others

reached into my soul and gave me peace

and then i wanted the same from God and began to pray

for God to be as compassionate toward me

as i was to others.

3.
the gravity is—

when i fell forty feet down a narrow steep hiking trail

and fell hard and tumbled without being

able to stop until i reached

bottom

i was not divinely protected

as i gradually healed i began to see

that the deeds of my compassion

toward others were my own

way of peace and that it

moved God not

to protect

me from

a fall.

4.
the truth is—

whether God cares for us if we care for others

is not reason enough for me to care or not

i care for others because the act itself gives me peace

whether God cares for us or not

my life is defined by how i treat others

it gives me a purpose and a meaning and

is not governed by how i perceive God treats me.

5.
more truth is—

despite my disappointment in my effort to convince God

to answer my prayers

   —an inner sense of God is in me

the terms of how God is

   —are revealed in the evidence

my peace is evident in how i treat others

   —and truth unfolds with the evidence it produces.

Dare Me Not

cloudy day
energy high
cool breeze

     i dare me
     to look your way

i straighten up
stretch my
back
and gaze
at the spot
where you
stand

     i dare me
     not to stare too long

people crowd
the park

the festival
is alive

i must make my
move

my eyes are glued
to you

The Observer

i dare me
to look your way

and patiently wait
for you to look mine

a strange mix of defeat and victory

—*male egos complex in thought
and yet simple-minded in action.*

Misguided Gratitude

i am grateful to my God
my gratitude has planted the seeds of my faith

i have built temples and written books
and i have died a thousand times defending my God

i am compelled to prove to myself that my God
approves of me for these acts

but the anguish i feel is because my neighbor believes not as i
because in his view i am an enemy to his God and
because his God requires him to defend Him from me

it is true my God and my peace are an insult to him
and true that he desires me to worship his God
and i would have him worship mine

my neighbor also has temples and books of his own
and he has died a thousand times defending
his God as i have mine

and though we are both gracious toward our own God
this does not produce trust toward each other

> *as we each hold fast to our gratitude toward our Gods*
> *we also fuel a mistrust that can ultimately justify*
> *any action against any who believe in a different God*

> *i prefer a God who can show us how to solve our mistrust*
> *of others where our beliefs in God are concerned*
> *rather than to hold steadfast to a misguided gratitude.*

Untitled

1.
he bobs his head
blushes red
grins like he's got
a coat hanger
in his
mouth

he stares
embarrassingly
at the blonde-haired wonder
till he is
convinced
she is ignoring
him

why would
she care
if he lives
or dies

his
smile turns
depressed
as
he watches
her
leave the
room

he stands
alone
crowded in
by
people

deluded
he thinks
if she would
but want to
know me
she would
see in me
a soul deep
and eyes
that penetrate
and are kind

yet he
refuses
to admit
that it does
not really
matter

being young
he is
deaf and
dumb
to blonde-
haired
beauties

The Observer

i could warn
him that
too much of
red lips
pretty hips
and dyed blonde hair
will get him
nowhere.

2.
but he
continues
to look
hiding
the fact
that it would
be ok if
she were
a whore
because
he too is
a whore
wannabe

all he wants
is
one look
and one
chance
to hook up
what more
is there
at nineteen.

3.
then
one night
i see
he catches
her eye
(he read
how to
in a book)
and
they leave
together

he tells
me later
she had
big thighs
and the smell
of old flesh
but that
it didn't
matter

we rubbed
we hugged
we moved
not in rhythm
but it didn't matter
it was done in
a minute
or less
mystery
solved

he says
she ran off
quickly
because
that night
did not
matter
to her
either.

4.
we all get
lonely
and do
something
stupid
at least
once

for my friend
that night
was not
a victory
until the
act was
done

he
didn't care
that
he had
chased
an old cow
though he
was
a young
bull

all he said
in his
defense
was

i can sleep now.

What Will God Be Tomorrow

yesterday God was the sun and moon
today God is in me
tomorrow i know not what
God will be
perhaps it depends on where we are as to
what God will be

i lose myself in these kinds of thoughts
thinking about how God is not revealed
the same way to us all

—every generation and every culture views
God with different eyes

to think God allows this and to think God wills this
requires a paradigm shift in order for us to
believe we know what God thinks

if i worship God from my own vantage and God receives me
does He also grant the same privilege to everyone

if it is up to us to decide who and what God is
do we all have that right given to us by God

thereby trusting God to minister to each of us
according to our need

i guess this seems more feasible to me than all the other
ways we have conceived of God thus far.

The Need for Sacred

what i view as sacred
is that which gives meaning
and purpose to our lives

that which is sacred is that which we
value most in our lives as a
godlike arena

all that we defend and pursue with
compassion and diligence
is the sacred in us

it may be different in each of us
yet the need for a sacred endeavor
is in us all

> —*i decide and you decide*
> *what is sacred for each of us*
>
> *as if God places the need for sacred*
> *in us and then gives us free rein*
> *to form what is sacred to us*

can the mystery of God's way be known
if we only take the time to unravel ourselves farther

> —*we are part of the mystery.*

Elusive Calm

the
elusive
calm
of silent
meditation
shelters
me
as long as the
breath of life
is in the
breeze
but
come a storm
the
silent meditation
shelters
me not
so i have learned
to lean on
the will
of my spirit
to give
me
strength
to endure
the
storms
     —so it is

silent
meditations
are for
breezes
and
the will
of my spirit
is to
endure the
storms
　　　—both being gifts from God to minister to and aid my soul.

e-clouds

virtual clouds

not real

but closer than

you think.

Epiphany One

when
listening
is
preferable
to
speaking.

Epiphany Two

wake up

    restroom

        weigh
        myself

if the scale
shows
weight loss
it is a
spiritual
moment

if not
it is
certainly
not a
spiritual
moment.

Epiphany Three

if my kindness
to you
does not help
then you
need
something more than
i know how
to give.

Epiphany Four

1.
i am not obligated to
a friendship
if he or she is not able
to give
the friendship what i
want or need.

2.
not all friendships
are the same
some require us to make
the effort to be a friend
to someone who does not
know how.

3.
if i choose to be a friend to
someone in need
of a friendship then i must
set boundaries
and learn to be a friend
knowing that person is unable
to reciprocate.

4.
friendship is not always
only about oneself.

Epiphany Five

we are all imperfect in our
ability to give
     perfectly

perhaps our imperfect
acts of kindness
transcend
     our imperfection.

Offend God

offend God
i think not

we are arrogant
to think so

if any offense is
taken by God
it would be
in our thinking that we can
offend
God.

Lucky Me

if i am
free
to live
on earth
how i
choose
    —lucky me

if luck
best describes
how the
good things
in life
have happened
then
i am
humbled
by the fact
that i earned
them not

and if God
holds me
not guilty
for the
lines
on this
page
    —lucky me.

Fly

1.
fly
spirit
fly
take
my
dreams
high

hope
heart
hope
till
my
dreams
find
home

seek
mind
seek
a path
for my
dreams
to
take.

2.

*what should
i dream*

*what path
should i
seek.*

Good Questions

when does
thought
enter
the spirit

when does
emotion
inspire

when does
the body
transcend the
physical

—*good questions*
can draw us in
before we
know it.

Us

on this
earth
it is
up
to us

without
us
earth
would not
have to
suffer
us

perhaps
it is a
privilege
to be
of
earth

if so
take care
to know
to whom
and to what
we are
a burden

and for whom
and for what
we are
to care.

Choice

no choice
have we
to be
born

but choice
we do
have

to
care
about
the
world
we are
born
to.

Freedom, Righteousness, Choice

freedom
without
vision
is chaos

righteousness
without
equality
is cruel

choice
without
purpose
is aimless

> *if i fail to understand their foundation*
> *then i fail in their meaning.*

My Uncle

5'9"
220 lbs
double chin
wrangler jeans
boots
too big
a buckle
beady eyes sunk in
chewing tobacco-
stained teeth
and a grin that
makes you
sick
unaware of
his own
repulsive
nature

he
speaks
with a heart
unashamed
of his belief
that
mexicans
blacks
asians and
any others
of "color"
are less
than
he

and that
all other
whites
other than
those of
his own
town
are
dogs
to be
petted
and taught
to obey
—like
the blacks
mexicans
and asians

and
any who
don't
know how
to perfectly
form
a cow-
boy hat
are also
on the
outs
> not all wrangler-boot-
> wearing
> cowboy-hatted men
> are this way
> but
> my uncle
> is.

Georgetown Cemetery, Grant County, New Mexico

1.

four months out of the year
no one can get there

the clay road and the steep
climbs up and down
make the road
impassable

yet two hundred people died
and are buried there
not counting the
ones who
lived on

why did they make their stake there
no one could come in or out
for eight months of the year
they risked it all
for a gold claim
—why.

2.

on a clear dry day the road
is a scenic drive into
georgetown with
views around
every curve

i love the piñon and
scrub oak that share
space with the
yucca and
cacti

the skyline rolls with
the hills and the air
has a freshness
about it

did the beauty of the land compensate
when the living was hard and
only mules dared the
georgetown
pass

whether or not the settlers saw it
the way i describe

they must have seen it as a better place
than the one they'd left

but perhaps the georgetown
cemetery reveals
otherwise

> *my hat's off to the early settlers*
> *of georgetown.*

Takers of the Road

pass me
quick
then
turn
without
a signal

weave
through
traffic
without
thought
of
others

text and
talk and
drive
without
under-
standing
why not

take our
life
and
abuse
our
safety
until
it
happens

then
hire a
lawyer
to legally
lie
for you
to find
a way
out of
the
damage
you
have
done

you are the takers of the road
where others' lives are
in your way.

Terror

terror is a
fear
an anxiety
that
builds
in us
from
an
unjustifiable
injustice

terrorists
are
those
who
act upon
their
fear
to seek
to right
the injustice

terrorism
is an
act of
terror
and
an act
of
justifiable
response

to make
right
the injustice
done
to them
first

*there are no roses
to smell here.*

Maze

i have walked
the maze
of life
where
my youth
noticed not
the many
stops
and turns

later
when i
married
and had
children
i learned
to pause
at the
stops
and turns
with
caution
—that is
when
the maze
began
to speak
to me

in the
pausing
i learned
to
listen
to the
wisdom
of the
maze
and
how
not to
fear
the load
of my
family
and the
stops and
turns
and the
unpredictability
of life

now
that
i am gray-haired
and my
children
are gone
my
wife and i
muse
over
the years

we
have
peace
with it
all

     i am ready now to enter the next life
            —the next maze.

River Life

river
life
see how
she
bends
and
moves
with ease
over
sand

cottonwood
thistle
mesquite
lining the
banks
of
river
life

observe
her
she is
nature
and
she is
natural

observe
her
she
turns
and
rolls
over
rocks
she is
cool
in the
heat
and
she is
prayers
answered
during
drought
she
caresses
rain

observe
her
and
life
all
around
her

we can all
learn
from
river
life

she is
gracious
to
allow
us
her
shore
and
to share
what
she has
and
to trust
us to
leave
her
belongings
in good
condition
so the
ones
who
come
after
us
can have
the same
privileges
as
she
has given
us

look upon river life
with gratitude
and respect

she deserves nothing less.

Four Poems for Winslow, Arizona

1. You Take My Breath

painted desert
road 87
hopi hideaway
—you take my breath

quiet beauty
painted
upon rocks
and moon-light
silhouette
the sky and earth
unify
painting
a scene
no human
could match

desert gallery
you give wonder
to the hopi eye
i envy you
and the hopi
soul
—you take my breath

i sense
i am the invader
on this land

and i owe
some respect
if i am to travel
road 87

      sunrise wakes
      while
      hopi spirits
      rise with
      hopes for rain
      while
      dead spirits
      dance for favor
      from
      the gods

      if i travel here
      i must
      bow as well
      to any of the
      gods that
      reside
      in the hopi
      land

      i am lost here
      without a reason
      as to why i came

      painted desert
      road 87
      —you take my breath.

2. Sand In Our Eyes

sunny days
below the mesa
beyond the painted mountain
sand in our eyes
at the east junction of
winslow arizona

starry nights
cold biting breeze
moon bigger than elsewhere
sunrises and sunsets
catching travelers
unexpectedly
when they spend the night in
winslow arizona

not the least
of towns
but least remembered
none recall
the santa fe railroad main
none recall the
great
mexican ranches
or the harvey grand hotel
la posada
none recall the migration
of the hopi and
navajo
to a land now known as
winslow arizona

ghosts of history
haunt the land
of known places
their souls'
breath forever
upon earth

is it only the ghosts who
will remember this earth
below the mesa
beyond the painted mountain
where railroads met
great ranchers herded
eastern travelers
refreshed themselves
and indians were
marched
to die

are we the ones who live
who will not and cannot
remember the great
past of this land

are we to be known as
the ones who have
—*sand in our eyes.*

3. Where Are You Winslow

where are you
winslow

past glory
faded

no santa fe
main

no mexican
ranch

no hopi
songs

no navajo
dance

only one bronze
statue on the corner
to remember
winslow by

a rock band
named the *eagles*
wrote a song
take it easy
about
winslow
and though
the song
was a
hit

it shed no
light
on
the past glories
of the town of
winslow.

4. Navajo Man of Winslow, Arizona

1.
sun-dried
carved
by sweat and
dry heat
face still
and eyes
deep
look my
way

did those
eyes see
me and
wonder
about me
as i did
them.

2.
navajo man
eighty-eight
so i'm told
eyes as
deep as
desert
horizons
a smile
like rain
water
found
atop
a
mesa.

3.
his stare
spoke to
mine
—*i am not one*
but many.

Witch's Errand

whirlwind
came
at me
like a witch's
errand
carrying
thorns
and dried
branches

whirlwind
came at me
descending
toward me
from
nowhere

i
her
target
she
filled
my eyes
with dirt
my hair
with grit

who is this
witch who
has sent
her
warning

i know
her

    —but i name no names
    in case she hears me.

A Fancy Vanity

men and their
beards
an obsession
untold

from a
distance
a man's
beard
seems
natural
but from the
mirror's
point
of view
      —a fancy
      vanity it is

a male's
time
in front of
a mirror
should be
less than
one-quarter
of an hour

but a man's
beard
is his best
kept
secret

that looks
make the
man
    —a fancy
    vanity it is

the time it
takes
to groom
a beard
into
the desired
look he wants
qualifies
as
a fancy
vanity

    —half an hour
    at the least
    for sure.

Gentle in the Night

gentle in the night
my dreams of you
awaken a desire
that wrestles with
my conscience

i wake to find myself
exhausted knowing
my dreams search
for you every night
  —we are lovers there
  you and i

do i dare tell you
of my dreams
do i dare ask you
if i am your lover
in yours

is it better to dream
in perfection than
seek rejection
in this reality
  —we are lovers there
  you and i

  so i will dream of the place
  where you love me
  and i love you

for what is the difference
between a dream and
this reality
if the bearer cares
not where his hopes
come true.

Where Did the Time Go
A ballad to an elder friend

1.

where did the time go

the past is gone

my kid's kids and their kids are all grown

at ninety i am moving slow

where did the time go.

staring at an empty sky

my memories

are re-lived by staring at an

empty sky

where did the time go.

2.

i am ready now to take

the journey

this is the only way i can

tell you

what it is i have been trying

to tell you

where did the time go.

my children's love though

true

does not fill my every

void

my life now empty without the one

i loved most

where did the time go.

3.

hold me tight and then let

    me go

my son my daughter know

    the best

of life is when we see that

    tomorrow

can be better than

    today

but for me that time has

    passed

where did the time go.

i am ready now to take

    my leap of faith

i am ready now let me go

    sorrow not

for it is a greater sorrow for me to stay

    than to leave this way

where did the time go.

4.

standing on the edge of a third-story house

    i jump

the time it takes for me to balance

    on the rail

and jump is maybe ten seconds

    and the time

i am in the air maybe two

    where did the time go.

Been Awhile

been awhile

    yeah it has

tell your wife
i said hello

    yeah
    it's been awhile

imagine all these years
living here
without bumping into each other
and then
bumping into each other
like this

    yeah

oh there's john
i gotta go
sorry

    well
    see you around

yeah
see ya.

Pooh

it seems there is no known universal meaning to life
that would satisfy us all in the same way

all the evidence points toward each of us
having to find a meaning that satisfies us individually

yet curiously we have no agreement that allows us to pursue
our own meaning and purpose freely

and we have no real universal teaching about how to approach
and live out these meanings to our lives

so we are left to fend for a meaning for ourselves and
to contest one another for our freedom to pursue that meaning

if God has a universal meaning it is that we all need
a meaning to our lives

—and that God offers no real protection against all the other
meanings to the other lives that may conflict with our own

it's a lot of pooh to contend with if you ask me.

Godis

just in

—godismagneticenergy

andwehavetogiveitaname

thesameaswedowithspacesbetweenwords

theonlywaywecanunderstandanythingistoarrange
itinawaythatwecanunderstandit

sowearrangemagneticenergytobegod
andweputspacesbetweenwords.

Short Life of Melinda

a neighbor i never knew

melinda
born at full moon
above purple skies
born in the late evening
of midnight

—no one exactly knew when

> *as her life only spanned*
> *a moment in time*

call melinda home
she is of the lost in the universe
back and forth she is swept
by the wind of the stars

—every which way

> *her birth gave her no time*
> *to make earth her home*

she is a blue bird
flying into free thought

she is yellow
autumn leaves falling

she is a deer
drinking from a cold creek

—*she is beauty that has no thought of a tomorrow*

    born of the full moon
    swept by the universe
    flying to nowhere
    falling always
    drinking without caution

    melinda came into the world
    and left before the day could
    collect enough wisdom
    to record her time

—*she is eternity's child*

    born to live seconds on earth
    and born to live forever as a
    child of the universe.

Storms and Snakes

storms
come
prepared
or not

my love
left
me for
another

and i think
they will not
be prepared
for the
storm
i bring

but also beware
　　—if you
　　tread on
　　the unhappiness
　　of a vulnerable
　　hurting
　　lover

　　you may also
　　be treading atop
　　the
　　snake

not
counting on
the storm
that's
sure to
follow.

A Truth Changed Me at Twelve

i remember well one day when i was twelve
walking along a dirt road and
seeing a hawk

i followed the hawk until i saw a raven
and chased after the raven until i
saw an owl at about dusk

i followed the owl until the moon
was out and full

and then i heard a voice in me say

> *you are not a hawk*
> *you are not a raven*
> *you are not an owl*

> *you are as special to me as they are*
> *you have wings of your own*
> *do not follow after their*
> *wings*

from that day on
i was not the same

i have not looked back
and i have not chased after
the wings of another.

Thank You for the Poetry

sun sets
at 8:00

breeze
slight

sky turns
orange

then
violet

the idea
of God

begins
to form

i have
an urge

to thank
God

then i lose
time

it is now
midnight

*i will not
hesitate
any longer*

*—thank you God
for all the poetry
and the years of
You and i.*

About Poetry and Poets

poetry

is depth
without boundary
without taboo

poetry

is lost in the writing
but without the writing the living it
could not be preserved and shared

despite the words' imperfection
poetry moves hearts and minds

poetry

is its own concoction
its own risk

it is a dare
and it has saved us
many a time

poetry

is not easy to read
so why does the poet
write it

because it is the nature of poetry
and the nature of the poet.

.

About the Author

Tony Prewit was born in Stamford, Texas in 1954 and then moved with his family at the age of eight to Silver City, New Mexico. He has earned both bachelor's and master's of arts degrees and has traveled extensively throughout the United States as a musician. Besides his interest in poetry, the author has written, directed, and performed in several plays and as a mime actor. In addition, he is an artist who delves in photography, charcoals, pastels, and watercolors. Art is his private therapy.

For over thirty-five years the author kept a jounal of poetry that chronicled his most secret, inner struggles with his belief in God. During that time he lived what seemed to be a fairly normal life—traveling, going to school, marrying, and owning a retail furniture company. This journal, however, does not chronicle his "normal" life, but his struggles with belief. He believes many people have these same kinds of inner challenges with life, and this journal brings to the forefront the reality of these challenges.

Since 1978 he has lived with his wife Pat, a classical pianist, in Silver City, New Mexico, the place he considers home for its culture, land, seasons, and people.

www.ingramcontent.com/pod-product-compliance
Lightning Source LLC
Chambersburg PA
CBHW052005090426
42741CB00008B/1562